Admission to higher education

A select annotated bibliography

Compiled by
**Bruce Choppin and
Patricia Fara**

NFER

Published by the National Foundation for Educational Research
in England and Wales

Registered Office: The Mere, Upton Park, Slough, Bucks, SL1 2DQ

Book Publishing Division: 2 Jennings Buildings, Thames Avenue,
Windsor, Berks, SL4 1QS

First Published 1972

© *B. Choppin and P. Fara, 1972*

SBN 901225 89 4

Cover design by
PETER GAULD, FSIA

Reproduced photolitho in Great Britain by
J. W. ARROWSMITH LTD., BRISTOL 3

Contents

Introduction

The pressure for university places increased dramatically during the 1950s, as more and more people reaped the benefits of an improved system of secondary education and an increase in the grants provided by the central government and local education authorities. Selection of students rapidly became a serious problem, with only about 60% of qualified school-leavers gaining admission to university by the time the Robbins committee was set up in 1961. The committee devoted considerable attention to the problems of selection, and the report (1963) recommended that the use of objective tests - similar to the American Scholastic Aptitude Test - and of a more structured system of school reporting be investigated. Research is still being carried out in these two areas and over the last ten years other research projects have focussed attention on the serious defects of our current selection procedures. In spite of the formation of the Universities Central Council on Admissions (UCCA) it is still true that choosing a student for a university place is a time-consuming and often apparently arbitrary process which may well result in the rejection of an equally suitable candidate. The importance of personality and social factors has also been investigated, but results in America would suggest that this is of little use in rationalizing the admissions system.

Until fairly recently, many people have tended to associate further education with universities, where most of the research has been carried out. The majority of references in this bibliography therefore, concern universities, although many of the results and comments are equally applicable to all areas of the higher education sector. Some general works have been included on polytechnics and colleges of further education. The extensive literature dealing with the prediction of teaching success has not been considered.

The book has been divided into several sections in the hope of guiding the individual reader to his particular interest. The first contains some standard reference books and general articles on the higher education system, and also a few guides for teachers and applicants about the different courses available. The general problems and effects of selection and wastage are covered in the next section, while the following two sections consider separately the functions of examinations and non-intellective factors in the selection process.

Although the British system of higher education is unique, much of the work done abroad is relevant, particularly American studies into the use of objective tests. The more interesting of these are included in the final section, together with information on research carried out in other countries.

Section I: The higher education system

The whole pattern of higher education in this country has changed radically over the past 25 years. The 1950s saw a growing demand for university places as secondary education was improved and financial aid increased, with simultaneous development of the technical colleges. In 1961 the Robbins committee was appointed to review the structure of full-time higher education and make recommendations to the government about long-term policy. The scope of the committee's enquiry was restricted to higher rather than further education, and the report concentrated on the universities. Nevertheless, the Robbins Report had a terrific impact. Proposals were made to more than double the percentage intake to university by 1980, and this was to be made possible by building new universities and by according university status to the Colleges of Advanced Technology. But the estimates of the Robbins Report fell short, and competition for university places has become keener than ever. The labour party's binary policy, by which polytechnics are empowered to award degrees, while the teacher training colleges are kept under the LEAs has further altered the face of higher education in this country. In addition, the foundation of the Open University represents a step in rather a different direction, but so far there is very little information about its success.

This section is a collection of books and articles about various aspects of the higher education system in Britain. The books by Peters provide a detailed account, with extensive bibliographies. A few articles have been included which look at the problems of degree courses at polytechnics, and also one on the Open University. The CRAC degree course guides are highly recommended for prospective students and teachers, since they provide extensive information about both universities and polytechnics and are very lucidly written.

1. ASKHAM, J. (1971)' Doing a degree at technical college (1): who does and why' Educ. Res., 1£, 2, 151-4.
A description of research carried out in 1966/67 by the Advisory Centre for Education (ACE) to compare the working of their own clearing house scheme for applicants to technical college with that of the DES, and to study the qualifications and motivations of the degree course students. The analysis is based on questionnaires received from 544 applicants through the ACE scheme and 220 through the official scheme, 257 students who had just completed their first year of a degree course at

technical college, and 30 in-depth interviews.
It appears that information on these courses is extremely hard for the prospective student to obtain, schools in particular providing far more help to university applicants. University students are broadly similar to those in this sample with respect to age, sex, social class and type of schooling, but far higher proportions of them had three rather than two A level passes, and the grades obtained were also much higher. The technical college degree course was shown to be a second-best alternative for students already strongly motivated towards obtaining a degree.

2. ASKHAM, J. (1971) 'Doing a degree at Technical College (2): attitudes of students', Educ. Res., 13, 3, 226-9.
    A continuation of the research described above, to investigate the attitudes of the same samples of students towards technical colleges. In their first term, 27% felt that technical colleges have no advantages compared with universities, their complaints focussing on the poorer facilities and lower teaching standards rather than on the higher status accorded to a university degree. In contrast with those following arts and social science courses, the students of science and technology felt that the colleges rather than the universities should be expanded to cater for technologists and the less able students. The attitude towards the technical colleges had generally become more favourable by the end of the year, the chief disadvantage now being seen as the poor social and cultural life.

3. BURGESS, T. and PRATT, J. (1970) Policy and Practice. London: Allen Lane (236 pp.)
    A study of the Colleges of Advanced Technology, concentrating on the ten-year period (1956-65) which saw their development from local technical colleges to autonomous universities. Numerous tables and graphs illustrate the text, which focusses attention not only on the students and courses but also on the topics of finance, staff and buildings.

4. BUTCHER, H. J. (1969) 'An investigation of the 'swing from science' '. Res. in Educ., 1, 38-57.
    Against the background of the Robbins and Dainton reports, an analysis was carried out in twenty schools to find out how early a leaning towards the arts or science sides is developed. Thirteen-year-old children showed clearly differential aptitudes and interests, which appeared to be more readily assessible than is generally supposed. Science specialization starts at an early age, but if this were changed, the indications are that the swing away from science would be maintained.

8

5. DEPARTMENT OF EDUCATION AND SCIENCE and CENTRAL OFFICE OF INFORMATION (1971). After A levels. London: HMSO (25 pp.) .
A liberally illustrated booklet concentrating on presenting to sixth-formers information on courses of full-time education outside the universities.

6. CAREERS RESEARCH AND ADVISORY CENTRE (1968). Upper School Choice. Cambridge: CRAC.
A booklet to help fifth-formers decide between going into employment, the sixth-form or a college of further education. After a general discussion, which includes details of further informative books, the problem is approached from two different view-points: necessary qualifications for a particular career, and the career options available with different A level combinations.

7. CAREERS RESEARCH AND ADVISORY CENTRE (1971). Yearbook of Education and Training Opportunities 1970/71. Professional Qualifications: Vol. 2. Cambridge: CRAC for Confederation of British Industry (190 pp.).
Information on over 1,000 advanced (non-university) courses in 74 colleges and polytechnics in the United Kingdom. For each institution, details are given about the courses offered together with the entry qualifications required. There is also a list of colleges within course, and a brief description of polytechnics and the CNAA.

8. CAREERS RESEARCH AND ADVISORY CENTRE. Degree Course Guides. Cambridge: CRAC.
A series of booklets with about 50 different titles, including 'Arts Degree Choice' and 'Science Degree Choice'. Updated about every two years, they provide comparative information about courses offered at different universities and technical colleges. They contain a large amount of extremely useful information which would be difficult for an individual student or teacher to collect.

9. CRAMPIN, A. (1969) 'Forecasting student numbers in higher education'. In: Research into Higher Education 1969. Papers presented at the fifth annual conference of the Society for Research into Higher Education. London: SRHE.
Given the failures of the predictions of the Robbins Report and the difficulties of isolating demand from supply, a project is described which attempts to trace the progress through the educational system of successive cohorts of 14-year-olds.

10. CRAMPIN, A. and ARMITAGE, P. (1970) 'The pressure of numbers: speculation for the seventies', Higher Educ. Rev., 2, 2, 5-14.
The estimates of the Robbins Report soon fell short of actuality, and this, coupled with the great increase in pupils staying on at school after 16, indicates a further escalation in the numbers applying for full-time higher education over the next decade. The financial implications are considered, together with the need for a reappraisal of the structure of the higher education system.

11. GOVERNMENT SOCIAL SURVEY (1970) Sixth-form Pupils and Teachers. London: Schools Council. (500 pp.).
The report of a survey carried out by interviews in 1967 on 4,377 sixth-formers and 1,302 teachers at 154 schools in order to investigate the courses and objectives in sixth forms, the background and future plans of the pupils, and the reactions of both pupils and teachers to the sixth-form experience. The text, accompanied by numerous tables, includes discussion of the effects in schools of university entrance requirements.

12. GOVERNMENT SOCIAL SURVEY (1970) Students in Full-time Courses in Colleges of Further Education. London: Schools Council (367 pp.).
The report of a survey carried out by interviews in 1968 on 4,540 full-time students of sixth-form age in 131 different colleges of further educati in order to study their courses of study, attitudes and ambitions, and compare them with pupils in sixth-forms at schools. Topics covered include the social and educational background of the students, their future plans and career choices, and their opinions on the educational system.

13. HEAP, B.W. (1971) A Survey of University Offers 1970/71. London: Cornmarket Press with National Association of Careers Teachers. (208 pp.).
This survey is intended to help the teacher in advising university applicants on which courses and universities to choose. The patterns of university selection procedures are analysed, but the main part of the volume consists of about 1,800 case histories of different applicants in 1970/71. These are grouped by subject of study, and the following information is given for each person: sex, country of residence, A and O level results (actual or estimated), applications through UCCA (course, university, order of preference), with the results.

14. ILIFFE, Alan (1969) 'Are sixth-formers old enough for university?' Times Educ. Supp., July 11, No. 2825, 13.
A general discussion of the far-reaching questions raised by the experience at Keele University of a multidisciplinary foundation year.

15. LAYARD, R., KING, J. and MOSER, L. (1969) The Impact of Robbins. Harmondsworth, Middx: Penguin.
A highly informative and readable evaluation of the successes and failures of the Robbins Report, ccvering such topics as university expansion, the binary system, and the swing from science. There are numerous tables and graphs.

16. MARRIS, P. (1964) The Experience of Higher Education. London: Routledge and Kegan Paul. (220 pp.).
A study originally undertaken for the Robbins committee, in which information from about 400 intensive interviews with undergraduates from three universities and a CAT is used to study the nature and content of higher education and how it appears to the student - both inside and outside the lecture theatre. The text is supported by numerous quotations and tables.

17. OXTOBY, M. and SMITH, B. M. (1970) 'Students entering Sussex and Essex Universities in 1966: some similarities and differences', Res. in Educ., 3, 87-100.
A factor analysis of answers to questionnaires completed by first-year students at Sussex and Essex, which aims to compare them in terms of their ideals and attitudes rather than their educational attainment. Rather few differences are found between the two universities, but seven interpretable factors are obtained, such as 'tolerance of ambiguity and uncertainty' and 'interest in theoretical approaches', which point to differences between faculties.

18. OXTOBY, R. (1971) 'Educational and vocational objectives of polytechnic students', Univ. Quart., 26, 1, 84-95.
A survey of nearly 150 first-year male students at Portsmouth Polytechnic on scientific degree courses. Their educational and social background is briefly discussed and compared with that of university students. The aims and expectations of the students, and their reasons for entering the polytechnic, are analysed in terms of course of study, entry qualifications, and previous experience.

19. PETERS, A. J. (1967) British Further Education. Oxford: Pergamon Press.
A 'text-book' account and analysis of British Further Education discussing its structure, aims, successes and failures. This is not just a description of English universities, but a factual appraisal covering four main sectors: vocational (technical, agricultural, commerce and art); part-time attendance for people under eighteen, adult education and youth service.

11

20. PETERS, A. J. (1967) <u>A Guide to the Study of British Further Education.</u> Slough: NFER.
A comprehensive account of published works - mainly government publications, reports of committees and conferences, and individual studies - about British further education. A useful reference book indicating how to obtain further information.

21. PRATT, J. (1971) 'Open University', <u>Higher Educ. Rev.</u>, 3, 2, 6-24.
A critical account of the establishment of the Open University. The first year's intake is analysed and compared unfavourably with the original objective 'to provide opportunities... of higher education... to all those who... have been... excluded from... an existing institution'. The failures of the Open University are traced back to the academic middle class concept of equating 'Higher Education' with 'University' and suggestions are made for methods of genuinely increasing the educational opportunities available to the working class.

22. REGIONAL ADVISORY COUNCILS FOR FURTHER EDUCATION IN ENGLAND & WALES. <u>A Compendium of Advanced Courses in Technical Colleges</u> . London: The Regional Advisory Councils in England and Wales.
Published annually. Under broad subject headings, such as 'Commerce and Management' and 'Science', lists are given of the different full-time degree, HND, diploma and sandwich courses in polytechnics, colleges of technology, agriculture, art and commerce. Information is also given about the course duration and entrance qualifications.

23. ROBINSON, E. E. (1968) <u>The New Polytechnics</u> . London: Cornmarket Press. (200 pp.).
A survey of the developments in further education since the war, analysing the effects and implications of the Robbins Report and the binary system. The present role of the polytechnics is discussed, but a new and more fundamental appraisal of tertiary education is called for.

24. SMITHERS, A. (1971) 'Students' experience of thick sandwich courses', <u>Educ. Res.</u>, 13, 3, 171-184.
A review of research on thick sandwich courses (in which the first two years are spent in university, the next in industry, and the final year in university) and the results of a survey at Bradford CAT to investigate students' attitudes towards industrial training. Although the sample sizes are rather small (15, 18 and 47) the results are in line with other work indicating that these courses are not attaining the objectives outlined by the NCTA.

25. VENESS, T. (1962) <u>School Leavers, Their Aspirations and Expec-</u>
    <u>tations</u>. London: Methuen.
    An account of an inquiry carried out in 1956 to study school-leavers'
    ambitions by tests and questionnaires. Topics covered include the
    family, work, motivational patterns and adolescence.

Section II: Selection and wastage

The problems of selection and wastage are inextricably mixed. As selection procedures improve, one would expect the number of unsuccessful students to fall, but this is only true to a certain extent. The evidence shows that the wastage rate has remained fairly constant at an average of about 13%-14% over the past 20 years in British universities. Many unpredictable factors, such as ill health or a diverting social life, mean that not all entrants to higher education will complete the course. The present selection system often results in rejecting as many potentially successful students as unsuccessful ones. Contemporary writers tend to place more emphasis on identifying the weaker student once at university, rather than further refining the selection procedure.

This section contains only general discussions of the selection problem, and more detailed accounts of particular research projects are found in the rest of the book.

Miller's book is by far the most comprehensive treatment of selection and wastage in Britain, and Heywood's paper provides a good overview of the problems of withdrawal.

26. ABERCROMBIE, M. L. J. et al. (1969) Selection and Academic Performance of Students in a University School of Architecture. London: Society for Res. into Higher Education.
A study of applicants to an architecture school from 1960-68, including a follow-up in 1963 of 272 who went elsewhere. Performance is related to actual selection criteria, such as previous attainment and interview, and to supplementary information based on the AH5 intelligence test and the Dynamic Personality Inventory.

27. ALBROW, M. C. (1967) 'Ritual and reason in the selection of students', Univ. Quart., 21, 141-151.
Selection by interview is extremely time-consuming and several research workers have demonstrated its inefficiency. In the view of the author, aptitude tests would have an undesirable educational backwash and so the increased use of A level results, the best single predictor currently available, is recommended. The role of the university is discussed and a scheme is outlined for centralizing and computerizing university admissions.

14

28. DAVEY, A. G. and RANDELL, G. A. (1971) 'Ways of improving the
selection of students', Univ. Quart. , 26, 1, 66-76.
A realistic appraisal of the whole procedure of selecting students for
university. Accepting that complete success is impossible, concrete
suggestions are made for improving selection methods within the
current system.

29. DREVER, J. (1967) 'Supplementary predictive information for university admission'. In: Research into Higher Education 1967. Papers
presented at the Third Annual Conference December 1967. London:
SRHE.
A discussion of the need for aptitude tests and school reports to
supplement GCE information about university candidates is followed
by a description of the project to evaluate Oliver's Test of Academic
Aptitude.

30. FEAGINS, W. (1968) 'Wastage in British universities', Educ. Res. ,
11, 1, 48-53.
Some statistics of wastage at different universities are presented,
followed by a critique of the system of university examining. Recommendations are made for increased staff/student contact and guidance
for those who have failed.

31. FINNEY, D. J. (1962) 'The statistical evaluation of educational allocation and selection', J. Roy. Stat. Soc. , Series A, (general) 125,
525-64.
A description of a theoretical model of university selection in Britain,
based on the two stages of entering and leaving secondary school.
Given that a fixed proportion of the total age-group is admitted to
university, the author discusses the methodology by which allocation
parameters should be fixed for different selective processes.

32. HEYWOOD, J. (1971) 'A report on student wastage', Univ. Quart. ,
25, 189-237.
An extensive review of the research and literature relating to student
wastage, with a bibliography containing some 130 entries. After a
survey of the problem, including a section on the difficulties of prediction and selection, the factors affecting withdrawal and some of the
remedies, are considered.

33. KELSALL, R. K. (1963) 'University student selection in relation to
subsequent academic performance'. In: HALMOS, P. ed. Sociological
Studies in British University Education. Keele: Univ. of Keele
(Sociological Review Monograph No. 7). 99-116
A critical appraisal of British selection procedures in universities.
Research is cited showing the low efficiency of selection and the

15

insufficient prognostic value of GCE results. The evidence indicates that objective tests are more reliable than interviews and school assessments.

34. KELSALL, R. K. et al. (1971) 'The young science graduate', Univ. Quart., 25, 3, 353-368.
An analysis of data obtained in 1966 by questionnaires from 2,690 men gaining their first degree in science at a British university in 1960. After a comparison with other graduates in terms of social class and degree characteristics, their later careers are discussed.

35. LOCKE, C. D. (1960) 'A record of student performance at Keele, 1950-58'. Univ. Quart., 15, 1, 46-53.
A study of the 1,250 students entering from 1950-1957 inclusively. The degree results and failure rates are compared with those at other universities and also internally from year to year.

36. LUMSDEN, T. (1959) 'Myths of prediction in university research', Educand, 3, 3, 275-6.
This short article points out that one cannot expect to obtain correlations about .5 between predictors and university attainment because of the low reliability of the criterion and the necessarily high degree of selectivity of any sample.

37. MILLER, G. W. (1970) Success, Failure and Wastage in Higher Education . London: Harrap for University of London Institute of Education. 264 pp.
An extremely extensive and thorough review of the literature, both British and foreign. The first four chapters cover the topics of wastage, student factors, student selection, and other institutional factors, while the last section, entitled 'Future Research Strategy', outlines the main directions which researchers should next explore both at the national and local levels.

38. PESTON, M. (1971) 'How can universities help comprehensive schools?' Compr. Educ., 19, 22-24.
A controversial article suggesting that a quota system for university admissions be established, so that places be made available in proportion to the percentages of pupils at different types of school. In this way, the importance of A levels would be diminished, and the comprehensive schools would not be forced to compete in a system which favours selective schools.

39. ROMANS, M. (1971) Building Degree Students: The Choosing and the Chosen , (Building Education Monograph), (93pp.) London: Polytechnic of Central London.
An investigation at Lanchester Polytechnic , Coventry, into the

applicants for the CNAA sandwich degree course in Building from 1966-1970. The social and academic backgrounds of successful and unsuccessful candidates are compared, and the subsequent progress of those accepted (a sample of only 96) is traced. Although no difference in performance is found between A level and ONC/D entrants, A level grades do seem to affect results.

40. SAINSBURY, A. B. (1969) 'Supplementary predictive information for university admission'. In: Research Into Higher Education. Papers presented at 5th Annual Conference of Society for Research into Higher Education in 1969. London: SHRE
A three-year progress report on projects inspired by recommendations in the Robbins report, to investigate the use of objective aptitude tests and of a more structured system of school assessment in selection for university.

41. VERNON, P. E. (1963) 'The pool of ability', In: HALMOS, P. ed. Sociological Studies in British University Education. Keele: Univ. of Keele. (Sociological Review Monograph No. 7).
Based on a memorandum submitted to the Robbins committee, this paper opposes the concept of a fixed 'pool' of intelligence, and recommends the use of objective type examinations and more research into the cultural and vocational background of university applicants.

42. WATTS, A. G. and DILLENBECK, D. D. (1969) 'A case for more information on university entrance standards', CRAC Journal, 4, 1, 7-10.
An explanation of how the current lack of information about acceptance at different universities and the structure of the UCCA system oblige teachers and pupils to play tactical games when filling out university application forms. Suggestions are made, based on the American experience, for helpful ways of presenting details about the selection procedures.

43. WESTLAND, G. (1971) 'Selection, performance and assessment', Univ. Quart., 25, 3, 344-352.
An attack on several fundamental principles underlying the selection and assessment controversy. The validity of aiming at perfect selection is questioned, as are conventional assessment techniques. Is obtaining a degree necessarily - or desirably - the sole criterion of success at university?

Section III: Examinations

The problem of selection is by no means a new one, and the traditional solution of formal written examinations was used as long ago as 1115 BC by the Chinese civil service. A level results have always been one of the main criteria for entry into the British further education system, although they are constantly attacked on several grounds. The inconvenient timing of the examinations, and the undesirable 'backwash' phenomenon, by which university entrance requirements are having an effect on school syllabuses long before the sixth-form is reached, could perhaps be excused if A levels were really an effective predictor of later performance. But all the research shows that this is not the case. Although results vary for different subjects, the general conclusion is that A levels correlate only poorly with subsequent examinations, the correlations decreasing as the time gap increases. In recent years, therefore, interest in Britain has focussed on more objective measures of achievement and aptitude, based broadly on the American example. However, research projects to date, including ones concerned with personality and motivation measures, all seem to indicate that although A level results fall a long way short of perfection, they do provide the best single predictor of university success.

This section presents most of the recent British research work on A level results and future university examinations, and many references to aptitude tests will be found in the last section.

44.   AUSTWICK, K. (1960) 'GCE to BA', Univ. Quart., 15, 1, 64-71.
A study of 245 students entering Sheffield University Arts faculty in 1954-6 who had taken three A levels in the summer immediately preceding their entry. Evidence was found that the A level standard has risen over the three years, perhaps because examiners maintain a constant pass/fail ratio. Correlations between degree class and A level results ranged from .13 (English) to .64 (French) but any reliable dividing line would be too high to be of practical value in student selection.

45.   BAGG, D.G. (1970) 'A levels and university performance', Nature, 225, 21 March, 1105-8.
Regression analysis is used to study GCE A levels and performance in university examinations, using data on students (mainly the 737 in chemical engineering) graduating from Manchester University between 1957 and 1969. Regression equations relating four different university

18

examinations and scaled A level marks show that the importance of
A levels diminishes with time and is negligible by the time Part II
finals are taken.

46. BARNARD, G.A. and McCREATH, M.D. (1970) 'Subject committ-
ment and the demand for higher education', J. Roy. Stat. Soc.,
Series A (general), 133, 3, 358-391.
An analysis of the data collected on 4,377 sixth-formers in 154 schools
by the Government Social Survey in 1967. University entry requirements are affecting subject combinations and school organization before
the sixth-form is reached.

47. BARNETT, V.D. and LEWIS, T. (1963) 'A study of the relation between GCE and degree results', J. Roy. Stat. Soc., Series A (general),
126, 2, 187-226.
A study of the GCE results and subsequent university performance of
some 1,300 candidates sitting JMB A level for the first time in 1956.
The pattern of degree results varied from university to university and
with sex, age and type of school. Prediction of degree result from
GCE grades together with age was achieved with a correlation of .40 -
.45.

48. COX, Roy (1966) Examinations and Higher Education : A Survey of
the Literature. London: SRHE (33 pp.).
A broadly historical study, supported by detailed analysis of about 60
references, of the development of examination techniques. The subject
is treated under the headings of traditional examinations, objective
examinations, the analytic approach, and anxiety and stress.

49. DALE, R.R. (1952) 'The prognostic value of the university entrance
examination', Brit. J. Educ. Psychol., 22, 2, 124-139.
A critical analysis of contemporary research reports from Scotland,
Australia and Sheffield is followed by an exposition of the difficulties
of prediction.

50. DALE, R.R. (1959) 'University standards', Univ. Quart., 13, 2,
186-195.
A discussion of the problems associated with university examinations -
their unreliability and the variations from department to department
and from year to year in the standard of any one degree class - leads
to the recommendation of the use of objective tests.

51. ELTON, L.R.B. (1969) 'The making of physicists', Physics Educ.,
4, 236-244.
An assessment of A levels and two specially designed physics examinations as predictors of university attainment, based on a sample of 397
honours physics students entering nine universities in 1964.

Correlation with degree result was higher for the total A level score (.35) than when calculated separately for physics (2.6) and mathematics (.28). Below the three B's level, A level results failed to have any predictive value. The advanced placement examinations in physics correlated only .19 and .23 with physics finals.

52.   FREEMAN, P.R.   (1970) 'A multivariate study of students' performance in university examinations', <u>J. Roy. Stat. Soc., Series A</u> (general), 133, 1, 38-55.
Several different techniques - including association analysis, component analysis, multiple regression and discriminant analysis - were applied to data on over 200 students in terms of about 60 variables derived from questionnaires and various personality and aptitude tests. The results indicate that A levels alone are insufficient as predictors of success in examinations which are themselves unstable.

53.   FREMER, J., COFFMAN, W.E. and TAYLOR, P.H.   (1968) 'The college board scholastic aptitude test as a predictor of academic achievement in secondary schools in England', <u>J. Educ. Measmt.</u>, 5, 3, 235-241.
The authors report the administration of a form of the SAT to 1,000 English grammar school children. There are some peculiarities in the sample as in some schools the fifth form rather than the sixth form was tested. The authors do not seem to understand the English system. In any case, the English group did quite well on the tests, scoring higher than did the American groups to which they were compared. Reliabilities similar to those obtained in the USA were found. Correlations with achievement scores were calculated, but no evidence of predictive validity is offered.

54.   GOULD, E.M. and M'COMISKY, J.G.   (1958) 'Attainment level on leaving certificate and academic performance at university', <u>Brit. J. Educ. Psychol.</u>, 28, 2, 129-134.
A follow-up of 674 Arts students at Edinburgh university in 1949/51 of relevance only in Scotland. Significant differences in attainment are found between entrants according to their achievement in the Scottish Senior Leaving Certificate examinations.

55.   NICHOLSON, R.J. and GALAMBOS, P.   (1960) <u>Performance in GCE and University Examinations.</u>   Hull: Institute of Education, University of Hull.
A survey of students in English, French, chemistry and economics at Hull University from 1954-57. Low correlations are found between degree results and A level.

56. NISBET, S.D. and WELSH, J. (1966) 'Predicting student performance', Univ. Quart. , 20, 468-80.
A follow-up of the 1961 arts and science intake at Aberdeen with a more detailed study of first-year performance. Since there are insufficient numbers to justify the use of correlations, cut-off techniques are tried out, leading to the conclusion that a cut-off point based on entry qualifications would exclude as many successful as unsuccessful students.

57. OLIVER, R.A.C. (1962) 'The selection of university students: a 'Scholastic Aptitude Test'?' Univ. Quart. , 16, 264-273.
A discussion of the drawbacks of the system of selection for British universities, and a description of the examinations set by the American College Board. The use in Britain of an objective examination based on the American Scholastic Aptitude Test (SAT) is recommended.

58. PETCH, J.A. (1961, 1963) GCE and Degree, Parts I and II. , JMB Occasional Publications, Nos. 10 and 14. Manchester: Joint Matriculation Board.
A study of about 3,000 university students taking A levels in 1956. Both A levels and degree results are grouped to provide 6 and 5 point scales respectively, and tables are supplemented by detailed discussions, often at the individual level, of discrepancies between the two examinations.   The sensible - if not very useful - conclusion is drawn that one can obtain 'reasonably certain knowledge of the...whole population ...without any certainty about how one specifiable individual is behaving now or will behave in the future. '

59. PHILLIPS, C.M. (1970) 'Some changes in the factors affecting university entry', Res. in Educ. ,   4, 81-94.
An examination of the effects due to the recommendations of the Dainton Report without any institutional changes actually having been made. DES and UCCA figures are used to compare the GCE patterns of university candidates in 1964 and 1967.   The connection between O and A level subjects is loosening, and more pupils (15% in 1967, 5% in 1964) are taking mixed A level courses with a consequent wider choice of university faculty. Streaming does not seem to be taking place in association with choice of sixth-form subject, but weaker students tend to apply for applied and social science courses at university.

60. PILKINGTON, G.W. and HARRISON, G.J. (1967) 'The relative value of two high level intelligence tests, GCE advanced level and 1st year university examination marks for predicting degree classification', Brit. J. Educ. Psychol. , 37, 3, 382-9.
252 students entering Sheffield University from 1955-63 to read psychology were given the AH5 intelligence test, and 153 of them also took Valentine's test.   A levels correlated better than either of these with

both the 1st year university examination (.24) and degree results
(.30). Regression analysis showed that the tests added little to A
level as a predictor. The authors conclude that research would be
more profitably concerned with temperament and personality factors
rather than cognitive ones.

61.   RICHARDS, J.P.G. and WILSON, A.J.C. (1961) 'A level and pass
       degree in physics', Univ. Quart., 15,   389-92.
       An inquiry carried out at Cardiff in the mid-1950s showing that the
       probability of obtaining a pass-degree jumps markedly from about
       .4 to about .7 at an A level mark of 55%.

62.   SHERWIN, E. and CHILD, D. (1970) 'Predicting the performance of
       undergraduate chemists', Educ. in Chemistry, 7, 4, 156-158.
       A study based on A level results of about 200 chemistry students
       entering Bradford University from 1964-67. Cut-off criteria correct-
       ly predicted the performance of 68% of the sample in the first year.
       There are brief discussions of degree results and of the ONC students.

63.   SIMONS, M. (1968) 'Qualifications of students on entry to colleges of
       education', Educ. for Teaching, No.75, 44-49.
       An analysis of the GCE results of students entering colleges of education
       in 1962 and 1963. Considerable differences are found between colleges
       when grouped according to sex, region and type of governing body. The
       effects on B.Ed courses and college applications are discussed.

64.   VALENTINE, C.W. (1961) 'The use of a new reasoning test for
       selection of university and training college students', Brit. J. Educ.
       Psychol., 3, 227-231.
       A test'for higher levels of intelligence' based on logical processes and
       inductive reasoning was given to 149 first-year students, 222 graduates,
       and 45 sixth-formers. Highly significant differences were obtained
       between the scores of candidates gaining different classes of honours
       degree.

65.   VALENTINE, J. (1967) 'GCE - a comedy and tragedy of errors',
       New Educ., 3, 2, 12-15.
       A highly readable American viewpoint of the strengths and failures of
       the GCE system, explaining the advantages of multiple choice tests
       such as the American Scholastic Aptitude Test (SAT).

Section IV: Non-intellective factors

The success of students depends not only on their academic ability but also on other characteristics. Numerous personality, motivation and values scales have been developed and related to performance in higher education. Eysenck's Personality Inventory with its neuroticism and extraversion variables has been widely used in British studies.

The selection procedure itself acknowledges the importance of personality factors by making use of interviews and school assessments, but the usefulness and reliability of these have been put seriously in doubt. More sinister perhaps, is the relationship between social class and academic success. While selectors would hesitate to use a personality measure as a predictor variable, many researchers - notably Furneaux - have shown that social background is already operating as a very effective selection criterion.

Apart from critical accounts of the selection procedures actually in operation, items included in this section have been restricted to those relating non-intellective factors to entry and success in higher education, and the numerous accounts of measurement scales and inventories have not been listed. All the American ones, and many of the British ones, can be found in Tests in Print, by Oscar Buros, or in the current volume of the Mental Measurements Yearbook.

66. BROCKINGTON, F. and STEIN, Z. (1963) 'Admission, achievement and social class', Univ. Quart. , 18, 52-73.
This survey of almost 1,600 students, carried out at Manchester University in 1957, finds pronounced differences in achievement between students from different backgrounds.

67. CAMPBELL, C.B. (1969) 'University admissions interviews don't just select applicants', CRAC Journal, 3, 3, 5-7.
A study of interviews of social science applicants at York University showed that, although the interview is not really a valid selective instrument, it does provide the means for a two way information flow between universities and prospective students. More efficient methods for this are suggested.

68. CHILD, D. (1969) 'A comparative study of personality, intelligence and social class in a technological university', Brit. J. Educ. Psychol. , 39, 1, 40-46.
A brief discussion of previous research is followed by an account of a sample of 607 students entering Bradford University in 1966 who

completed the Eysenck Personality Inventory and the Nufferno intelligence test and supplied further biographical information. These students from a technological university were intermediate in terms of extraversion and neuroticism between student and population norms. Appreciably higher scores were obtained on the intelligence test by the science and technology students than those following arts and social science courses. Proportionally more students originated from working-class homes than is the case in established universities.

69. CORTIS, G.A. (1968) 'Predicting student performance in colleges of education', Brit. J. Educ. Psychol., 38, 2, 115-122.
The predictive power of various cognitive, creativity and personality measures, together with biographical information, was analysed in terms of final examination results. 259 students in 1965 completed a five-hour test battery, and correlations and Varimax factor analysis were used to find factors relating to classroom and academic success. The results are compared with a similar investigation of students in university's Department of Education.

70. COUPER, M. and HARRIS, C. (1970) 'CAT to university: the changing student intake', Educ. Res., 12, 2, 113-20.
An analysis of almost 900 questionnaires completed by students at Bath University of Technology in 1966 in order to compare them with those of 1963, when the university was still Bristol College of Science and Technology. The changed status is reflected by the higher proportion of entrants from middle class rather than working class backgrounds, and also in terms of other variables such as parental support, entrance qualifications, and attitudes towards education.

71. ENTWISTLE, N.J. et al. (1971) 'Prediction of Academic Performance'. Lancaster: Rowntree Research Unit, University of Lancaster.
The first volume of a report entitled 'The social implications of educational change: a cross-institutional investigation into educational objectives and student performance in higher education'. An extremely well written review of previous research and literature gives the background of the many different variables chosen to describe each student. A rather unrepresentative sample for this preliminary report was used, comprising 898 students from three universities, 562 from four colleges of education and 190 from five polytechnics. They all completed questionnaires including biographical information, personality scales, motivation, attitude and value tests, and half of a test of academic aptitude. Attainment in the first-year examinations was used as the criterion variable, and correlation techniques and cluster analysis were used to analyse the characteristics of students following different courses at the three different institutions. Pronounced differences

were found not only in attainment on verbal and numerical tests, but
also in terms of personality (extraversion and neuroticism), study
methods, motivation and values (social, religious, aesthetic, etc.)

72.   ENTWISTLE, N.J. et al.(1971) 'Prediction from scales of motivation and
      study methods', Brit. J. Educ. Psychol., 41, 3, 258-265.
      A report on the development and validation of a British inventory to
      measure the motivation, study methods and examination technique of
      students in higher education.   The tests were taken by about 1,700
      students and although fair reliabilities were obtained (.79 after six
      weeks), and the scales correlated .77 with the Brown-Holtzmann
      American scales, correlations with academic attainment variables
      were low.   Reasons for this are discussed.

73.   ENTWISTLE, N.J. and BRENNAN, T.   (1971) 'Types of successful
      students', Brit. J. Educ. Psychol., 41, 3, 268-276.
      The application of cluster analysis to describe the different routes to
      academic success and failure of 875 university students.   The 23
      variables used for the clustering were chosen from the intellectual,
      personality, study-habits and values domains, and included the criter-
      ion variable of academic performance at the end of the first year.
      The clustering proceeded from 15 down to 2 groups, and the 12 cluster
      solution, judged to be the most satisfactory, was described.   No
      attempts were made to predict future performance by clustering on all
      the variables apart from the criterion variable.

74.   EYSENCK, H.J.   (1947) 'Student selection by psychological tests',
      Brit. J. Educ. Psychol., 17, 1, 20-39.
      A critical survey of British and American literature with an extensive
      list of references.   Experimental results and comments are treated
      under the headings of 'intelligence and success at college', and 'con-
      siderations regarding the use of selection tests'.

75.   FURNEAUX, W.D.   (1961) 'The Chosen Few'. London: OUP   (245 pp.)
      A ten-year research project was sponsored by the Nuffield Foundation in
      1948 to consider the problems of selection for university.   This account
      presents the results of the survey of 12,000 school-leavers in the con-
      text of other data on the educational system.   The importance of non-
      academic factors, such as social class, is stressed.   School-leaving
      examinations, although imperfect, prove to be the best single predictor
      of university performance, and the limitations of the whole selection
      procedure are discussed extensively.

76.   FURNEAUX, W.D.   (1962) 'The psychologist and the university',
      Univ. Quart., 17, 33-47.
      An exposition of the need to study not only the characteristics of the

student, but also the ways in which the university and the student may interact. Data are presented from the first and second year examination results of 91 engineering students, and used to obtain factors being measured by the examinations. The connections between university attainment, neuroticism, introversion and drive are discussed and related to the admissions problem.

77. FURNEAUX, W. D. (1963) 'The too few chosen and the many that could be called'. In: HALMOS, P. ed. Sociological Studies in British University Education. Keele: Univ. of Keele. (Sociological Review Monograph No. 7).
The author opposes the concept of a fixed 'pool of ability', showing that there has been little apparent change since 1953 in the social class distribution of school-leavers with at least two A levels. He suggests that if the handicaps associated with a working-class background, such as low educational motivation, could be overcome, then about 25% of an age cohort could reach matriculation level.

78. GAMMIE, A. (1964) 'The influence of a sixth form year in school on academic performance at University', Educ. Res., 6, 1, 77-9.
A study of the academic effect of a non-compulsory sixth year at school for the Scottish entrants to the Arts and Medicine Faculties at the University of Aberdeen in 1959 and 1960. The sixth-year entrants did rather better than the fifth-year ones in the examinations at the end of the first year, but the difference was small and not statistically significant.

79. HAMILTON, V. (1968) 'Scholastic and non-scholastic correlates of university students' academic performance'. In: Research Into Higher Education, 1967. Papers presented at Third Annual Conference of SRHE December 1967. London: Society for Research into Higher Education.
This study aimed to compare traditional predictive criteria with those derived from non-scholastic variables. In addition to correlations, regression and factor analyses were used, but the sample sizes were only 32, 62 and 169. Undergraduates at Reading University took a high-level intelligence test, and completed various personality and motivational questionnaires. Data were also collected from their UCCA forms and although the last school examination emerged as the best single discriminating variable, the UCCA scholastic/historic information was seen to be inadequate. The intelligence test offered no improvement, but the non-scholastic variables were shown to contribute substantially to examination performance.

80.   HAMILTON, V.   (1970)   'Non-cognitive factors in university students'
      examination performance', Brit. J. Psychol. , 61, 2, 229-41.
      A short review of the problems of university prediction is followed by
      a description of a study of 169 first-year students at Reading University
      in terms of 64 scholastic, intelligence, personality and motivation
      variables.   By adding up the numbers of significant correlations and
      differences between attainment in the first year university examination
      and the predictors, the A level examination is shown to be by far the
      most discriminating single variable.   It is suggested that any improve-
      ments in the prediction of students' academic performance may only
      be achieved by standardised operations involving differentially weighted
      multiple variables.

81.   HIMMELWEIT, H. T.   (1963)   'Student selection'.   In: HALMOS, P.
      ed. Sociological Studies in British University Education.   Keele: Univ.
      of Keele.   (Sociological Review Monograph No. 7).
      A description of two frequently quoted studies at LSE to evaluate ability
      and personality tests as predictors in comparison with existing selec-
      tion procedures.   Their value now seems to be more in the searching
      reappraisal of selection methods than in the actual data used and the re-
      sults obtained.   The first sample consisted of about 300 students of
      commerce, economics and social science who in 1945-47 were mainly
      ex-servicemen, and the second of about 700 students of economics,
      law and sociology in 1957-59.   Both projects indicate the usefulness of
      personality tests, and recommendations are made to set up regional or
      national centres to enable the universities to see not only the students
      in the context of all applicants, but also to compare departments in
      different universities.

82.   HOLDER, R. L.   (1970)   'Sex, social class, and student performance',
      Univ. Quart. , 24, 2, 166-172.
      A discussion based on data on 1, 633 applicants to read mathematics at
      Birmingham University from 1959-62.   For those accepted, significant
      sex differences are found both in A level achievement and school assess-
      ment.   The headmasters' rating of students varies with the social class
      of the parents.   Differences are also found with respect to both sex and
      social class in the post-school career of all the applicants.

83.   KLINE, P. and GALE, A.   (1971)   'Extraversion, neuroticism and
      performance in a psychology examination', Brit. J. Educ. Psychol. ,
      41, 1, 90-94.
      The Eysenck Personality Inventory was administered to 455 students
      taking the human development examination at Exeter University over
      a five-year period.   Correlations between academic performance and
      extraversion and neuroticism were computed for year groups as a

whole and for special groups. No stable pattern of correlations emerged, thus casting doubt on the contention that the mildly neurotic introvert succeeds best at university. There was no evidence either of curvilinearity of regression as suggested by other studies.

84.   MACLAY, I. (1968) 'A random sample of university undergraduates', Univ. Quart., 23, 1, 80-94.
A random sample of 166 students entering Birmingham University in 1964 was interviewed to explore the relationships between degree results and social, medical and academic history. A large number of variables was used, and although these cannot lead to completely successful prediction, χ^2 tests showed many of them to be significantly related to university performance.

85.   NEWFIELD, J. G. H. (1963) 'Some factors related to the academic performance of British university students'. In: HALMOS, P. ed. Sociological Studies in British University Education. Keele: Univ. of Keele. (Sociological Review Monograph No. 7).
A summary of some of the findings of the LSE national survey of about 6,000 students entering university in 1955. The sample comprised 1 in 2 of all medical students, 1 in 5 whose fathers were 'non-manual' workers, and 1 in 2 of those with 'manual' fathers. Tables are presented relating academic performance with sex, social class, secondary education, course of study, vacation work, accommodation and finance.

86.   NISBET, S. D. and NAPIER, B. L. (1970) 'Promise and Progress'. Glasgow: Univ. of Glasgow.
A study of 1,048 students at Glasgow University taking Scottish Highers in 1962. Statistical analyses are deliberately omitted, all results being presented as percentages, with the aim of making the work more useful to the general reader. Success is rated only on a dichotomous pass-fail basis, and related from questionnaires not only to academic attainment but also to rather qualitative variables such as 'keenness at time of entry to university', 'freedom from severe strain and worry over examinations', 'relatively easy transition from school to university'. Surprisingly, success is not found to be related to 'cultural richness of home'. A study is also made of the 'morale among Glasgow students and their parents in the 1960s and of the 'University and the community'.

87.   PETCH, J. A. (1964) School Estimates and Examinations Results compared. (J. M. B. Occasional Publication No. 21). Manchester: Joint Matriculation Board.
This comparison of over 2,000 A level results with the schools' estimates is essentially based on detailed descriptions of numerous

particular cases. The main conclusions are that: although schools tend to rate more highly, there is general agreement about the order of merit; highly differing assessments can be reconciled by realising that they are measuring different aspects of the candidates ability; the well-worn story about the good candidate being a poor examinee should be replaced by one about the examiners being falsely persuaded by a poor candidate that he merits a high mark.

88. WANKOWSKI, J. (1969) 'Some aspects of motivation in success and failure at university'. In: Research Into Higher Education 1968. Papers presented at 4th Annual Conference of the Society for Research Into Higher Education. London: SRHE.
A review of data from studies carried out at Birmingham University showing the importance of motivation in academic success, and analysing degree result in terms of goal orientation, extraversion and neuroticism and stress.

89. WARBURTON, F. W. et al. (1963) 'Predicting student performance in a university department of education', Brit. J. Educ. Psychol., 33, 1, 68-79.
100 teachers in the Manchester University Department of Education in 1957-8 were studied in terms of 100 variables to determine the relative efficiency as predictors of teaching success of personality and achievement factors, together with biographical information. Correlations and factor analyses led to the conclusion that successful teachers have a high general cultural level, are conscientious, and socially active.

90. WILSON, J. D. (1971) 'Predicting levels of first-year university performance', Brit. J. Educ. Psychol., 41, 2, 163-70.
The first year academic performance of 1,015 arts and science students at Aberdeen was compared with their school examination results and headmasters' assessments. Test scores of ability, personality profiles, motivation and study methods were collected for about half the sample. Variables significantly related to performance were treated as indicators of merit and symptoms of failure. Of those who actually failed, 80% had been put in the 'at risk' category. Research is suggested into the use of cluster analysis to provide a profile of candidates in terms of these variables.

Section V: Work in other countries

Although every country in the world is able to offer higher education (or tertiary education as it is being labelled in some places) to some young adults, none of them is yet able to offer it to all. The proportion of young people who receive education at a college level varies enormously from about 50 per cent in the United States to very much less than one per cent in many under-developed countries.

There are two quite distinct approaches to the selection problem. In some countries the many students completing secondary school compete for a smaller number of places in college, the selection being based on examinations or some method of continuous assessment of high school achievement. In other countries the selection occurs earlier. Economic and social pressures, and sometimes intellective criteria, serve to reduce the numbers in secondary education to such an extent that those who complete the course can be accorded a 'right of entry' to higher education. Britain lies somewhere between these two extremes, quietly rejecting many students during the secondary stage, but then admitting only about one half of those who theoretically qualify for a university education.

The entries in this section are just a small fraction of the vast amount of literature published throughout the world on admission to university. Those included have been chosen either because they themselves have extensive bibliographies (these are indicated by an asterisk), or because they are directly relevant to the problems of university entrance in the United Kingdom.

Most of the entries refer to American work. The main topics concern the Scholastic Aptitude Test (SAT) which has been the major criterion for college admission for several decades, and the way in which the admissions procedures work, particularly with regard to minority groups. Research into the use of aptitude tests is going on in several parts of the world. In Canada a test adapted from the SAT is in use experimentally, but no results have so far been published. More information is available about an Australian aptitude battery, although this too is in an early stage of development.

* 91.   ANGOFF, W. H. ed. (1971) The College Board Admissions Testing Program. New York: College Entrance Examinations Board.
An important account of the work of the major agency for college admissions testing in the United States. The board prepares and administers standardized achievement tests in a wide variety of subject areas as well as the better known 'Scholastic Aptitude Test'.
The book contains a historical survey of the evolution of admissions

testing, and of the particular development of the SAT. Technical details of the tests and procedures used for standardization are reported, and there is a summary of recent American research into the problems of selecting college students.

92. ASTIN, A.W. (1965) Who Goes Where to College? Chicago: Science Research Associates.
This reports a study of the 127,000 students that entered 248 selected colleges and universities in the autumn of 1961. Data on student abilities and interests is related to the characteristics of colleges and particularly to the range of courses offered. When the data was analysed, six factors characteristic of the student intake were found. Profiles on these factors are included for more than 1,000 colleges and universities throughout the USA.

93. BEAN, A.G. and CENTRA, J.A. (1970) Multiple College Applications, ETS Research Bulletin RB-70-2, Princeton: NJ: Educational Testing Service.
An investigation of behaviour patterns with regard to applications for admission to college in the United States. Discriminant analyses are used to describe groups who make various numbers of applications. Students who make more than one application have above-average SAT scores but are average in high school achievement.

94. BIGGS, D.A. and TINSLEY, D.J. (1970) 'Student-made academic predictions', J. Educ. Res., 63, 5, 195-7.
Three small samples of college freshmen were asked to predict their own ability to learn, and the results were correlated with their first year college grades, and previously obtained aptitude scores (ACT). Intercorrelations were all about 0.50. The authors conclude that this sort of information from students could be helpful to those concerned with arranging remedial programs.

95. BLOOM, B.S. and PETERS, F.R. (1961) Academic Prediction Scales. New York: Free Press.
Predictive correlations for success in college suffer from variations among high schools and colleges. When SAT scores are used to define scales, adjustments for both high school standards and college standards can be made, leading to an increase in prediction from about 0.50 to 0.75. The authors conclude that this will help both schools and colleges in finding appropriate places for students and thus reduce the rate of academic failure.

31

* 96. BOWLES, F. (1963) <u>Access to Higher Education.</u> 2 vols. Paris: UNESCO.
Volume 1 is a report by the director of the International Study of University Admissions set up in 1960 to study problems affecting the organization, operation and functions of institutions of higher education. It contains a concise account of university admissions processes across the world. Volume II presents detailed case studies of 12 countries (including Great Britain) with extensive bibliographic material.

97. CHAUNCEY, H. and HILTON, T. L. (1965) 'Are aptitude tests valid for the highly able?' <u>Science</u>, 148, 3675, 1297-304.
Yes. Studies of people with very high SAT scores show that the test remains a valid predictor of subsequent performance such as, for example, the gaining of a PhD degree. Other researches using various tests including the GRE and the MAT confirm this finding.

98. CLEARY, T.A. (1968) 'Test bias: prediction of grades of negro and white students in integrated colleges', <u>J. Educ. Measmt.</u>, 5, 2, 115-124.
Aware that the Scholastic Aptitude Test predicts about equally well for white and black students, the author questions whether it consistently over-predicts or under-predicts for either group. It had been suggested that the test is unfair to negroes. The study reported was confined to three 'integrated' colleges in the United States. No significant differences between racial groups were found in two cases, but in the third, test scores (and indeed high school averages) consistently <u>over-predicted</u> the achievement of negroes.

99. DANIELS, M.J.M. and SCHOUTEN, J. (1970). <u>The Screening of Students; Problems of Assessment and Prediction of Academic Performance.</u> London: Harrap for Council of Europe.
A theoretical discussion of university systems and the problems of selecting students for them. Some results from American research are quoted, but the reader may well feel that this small volume raises a vast number of questions without answering any of them.

* 100. FISHMAN, J.A. and PASANELLA, A.K. (1960) 'Colleges admission - selection studies', <u>Rev. Educ. Res.</u>, 30, 4, 298-310.
This review of American research prior to 1960 is fairly comprehensive and as it contains an extensive reference list itself, it is the earliest American source cited here. The hundreds of research studies considered showed that high school achievement and aptitude scores both correlate about 0.50 with first year college grades. Multiple correlations using both types of predictors average about 0.60. However, the correlations are much lower when the samples are restricted to very able students. Much work has been done on the use of non-intellective predictors such as personality traits, but little of practical value had emerged.

101. FRENCH, J.W. (1964) 'New tests for predicting the performance of college students with high-level aptitude', J. Educ. Psychol., 55, 4, 185-94.
Fifteen experimental tests were tried out in an attempt to improve the capacity of the College Board tests to predict college performance of students in very high-level colleges. The results suggest that sets of items on General Information and Insightful Reasoning would improve the validity of the SAT but only at some slight reduction in reliability.

102. GOSLIN, D.A. (1968) 'Standardized ability tests and testing', Science, 159, 3817, 851-5.
A wide-ranging survey of the current influence of standardized tests in American Education. The author points out the technical shortcomings of tests used for predictive purposes particularly for college admission, and also discusses the invasion of privacy that test-based selection procedures could provoke.

103. GREEN, R.L. and FARQUHAR, W.W. (1965) 'Negro motivation and scholastic achievement', J. Educ. Psychol., 56, 5, 241-243.
In this study samples of Negro and 'Caucasian' high school students were used to compare the efficiency of various test scores as predictors of overall academic achievement. The authors find that Verbal Reasoning is virtually uncorrelated with achievement for Negro males although a correlation of 0.62 is found for non-negro males. However, little information is given on the source of the data, and some of the statistical procedures used appear questionable.

104. HILLS, J.R. (1966) 'Diversity and the Effect of selective admissions', J. Educ. Measmt., 3, 3, 235-42.
During an eight-year period when the State of Georgia was having to be more selective in admissions to the state colleges, the author examined data on entering students to determine whether or not diversity within the system was diminishing. He concludes that during this period, variations of aptitude level within individual colleges increased, new types of college sprang up, and 'desegration' brought increased racial diversity.

105. KAYSEN, C. (1971) 'Higher education: For whom? At what cost?' In: Proceedings of the 1970 Invitational Conference on Testing Problems, Princeton, NJ: Educational Testing Service.
The author considers the limitations of the present structure of higher education in the United States, and recommends that it slowly develop into a two-tier system offering 3-year first degrees at the lower level and better facilities for advanced and professional work at the higher. This would greatly increase the opportunities for college education while protecting the high standards of certain institutions from the pressures

33

for an 'open admissions' policy.

106. LAVIN, D.E. (1965) The Prediction of Academic Performance.
New York: Russell Sage Foundation.
An important American work on the subject, this book provides a
theoretical analysis of academic prediction and an extensive review of
the research at all academic stages. After discussing the meaning of
academic performance and the problems associated with its measurement and prediction, Dr. Lavin studies four broad categories of performance determinants: intelligence and ability factors, personality
characteristics, sociological determinants and socio-psychological
factors. The final chapter recommends future research into the inter-
action of personality and social structure.

107. LEVIN, H.M. et al. (1971) 'School achievement and post-school
success - a review', Rev. Educ. Res., 41, 1, 1-16.
An American review of the current state of knowledge regarding the
extent to which future life patterns, earning capacities, social mobility
etc., are determined by school achievement. The importance of admission to college is discussed in this context.

108. LUNNEBORG, C.E. and P.W. (1970) 'Relations between aptitude
changes and academic success during college', J. Educ. Psychol., 61,
169-73.
An investigation of the predictability of performance at various points
of a four-year college course by pre-college aptitude and achievement
measures. Assessments of college performance were made quarterly
for a small sample of college students. For the first three years of
the course moderately good predictions were possible but the correlations shrank to near zero in the final year.

109. MILLER, G.W. (1970) Higher Education Research In Australia and
New Zealand. London: Society for Research into Higher Education.
This monograph summarizes a great deal of research material, much
of it not generally available in this country. Selection procedures are
more akin to those in Britain than to those in the USA although recent
dissatisfaction with the low correlations of school exam results with
college performance has led to experimentation with a battery of aptitude
tests.

110. MUNDAY, L. (1965) 'Predicting college grades in predominantly negro
colleges', J. Educ. Measmt., 2, 2, 157-60.
Munday studied the American College Testing Program test data for five
predominantly negro colleges and found that 'the ACT test scores oper-
ated with about typical predictive efficiency at these colleges.'
However, his analysis includes a major upward adjustment of correlation

coefficients due to the restricted range of negro test scores.
Stanley and Porter (qv) argue that this adjustment was not valid and
hence the results should be accepted only with caution.

111. NOVICK, M.R. et al. (1971) Applications of Bayesian Methods to the
Prediction of Educational Performance. ACT Research Report 42,
Iowa: American College Testing Program.
The authors demonstrate that stable regression equations can be drawn
from smaller samples when a Bayesian Statistical approach is adopted.
They suggest that this opens the way to use of statistical selection procedures for colleges with as few as 25 entering students in a given
course, whereas 100 students had hitherto been considered the mini-
mum.   Data from 22 small American colleges are used to demonstrate
the technique.

112. RECHTER, B.   (1970) Admission to Tertiary Studies. Melbourne:
Australian Council for Educational Research (Occasional Paper No. 2).
This book traces the development of a five component aptitude test for
use by the Australian universities, and discusses its potential applications.   The test battery, of which a sample is presented in the
appendix, is remarkable for the wide range of material and skills it
incorporates.   The test was first administered experimentally in 1968
and at the time of writing little evidence on validation is available.

113. RECHTER, B. and WILSON, N.L.   (1968) 'Examining for university
entrance in Australia: current practices', Quart. Rev. Austral. Educ.,
2, 2, 1-26.
This paper is mainly a detailed analysis and criticism of the 'matriculation' examinations, set on a state-wide basis which heretofore have
been the major criterion for acceptance/rejection of university applicants.   The authors call for greater objectivity in the future on the
part of those responsible for examinations.

114. RICHARDS, J.M. et al.   (1966)   The Prediction of Student Accomplishment in College , ACT Research Report No. 13, Iowa City: The American
College Testing Program.
The authors show that non-academic accomplishment in college can be
predicted from high school non-academic performance about as well as
college academic accomplishment can be predicted from high school
academic performance.   They also find that the two classes of accomplishment are largely independent, and argue for a broader view of
ability, and for college recruitment that would give more weight to non-
academic criteria.

115. SAVAGE, R.D. (1962) 'Personality factors and academic performance', Brit. J. Educ. Psychol., 32, 3, 251-3.
168 students at an Australian university took the Maudsley personality
inventory and the results supported British research findings in valid-
ating Eysenck's theories that neuroticism and introversion are posi-
tively correlated with academic success.

116. SEASHORE, H.G. (1962) 'Women are more predictable than men',
J. Couns. Psychol., 9, 3, 261-70.
A review of available American data leads the author to conclude un-
equivocally that 'Academic grades of women in high school and college
are better predicted from aptitude tests than are the academic grades
of men'. The causes of this phenomenon are not known.

117. STANLEY, J.C. and PORTER, A.C. (1967) 'Correlation of Scholastic
Aptitude Test Score with college grades for negroes versus whites',
J. Educ. Measmt., 4, 4, 199-218.
The authors conclude, after an extensive review of earlier research
and a careful analysis of results from their own 6-year study, that the
SAT predicts about as well for negroes as for whites. Multiple
correlations in their study (high school average, SAT-V and SAT-M)
run from 0.55 to 0.70 for negroes. The method of analysis is a com-
plex ANOVA design with colleges nested within races and crossed with
years. The dependent variable was a Fisher z-transformation of the
basic r. A comment is made that the correlations might be higher for
these students - all from the state of Georgia - if the SAT was easier.

118. STANLEY, J.C. (1971) 'Predicting college success of the education-
ally disadvantaged', Science, 171, 640-47.
An extensive review of the research carried out in the last decade into
the problems of unequal opportunity for higher education in the United
States. The author believes that there is overwhelming evidence to
suggest that aptitude-scores backed with high school achievement are
the fairest criteria for college selection, and that the admission of a
number of black students with very low ability can have very harmful
effects on these students, on the college itself, and on the educational
system as a whole.

119. TEMP, G. (1971) Test Bias: Validity of the Scholastic Aptitude Test
for Blacks and Whites in Thirteen Integrated Institutions. ETS Research Bulletin RB-71-2, Princeton, NJ: Educational Testing Service.
When SAT scores are used to predict first-year college grades for
blacks and whites separately, the regression equations produced are
significantly different. The finding is that if the majority group equa-
tion is used generally then the performance of black students will be
substantially overestimated. Unfortunately, the statistics used in this
study, particularly the assumptions of linearity, are open to question.

Author index